I Spied an

ACCORDION

I Spied a

BASKET

I Spy with my Little Eye Something beginning with...

I Spied a

DONUT

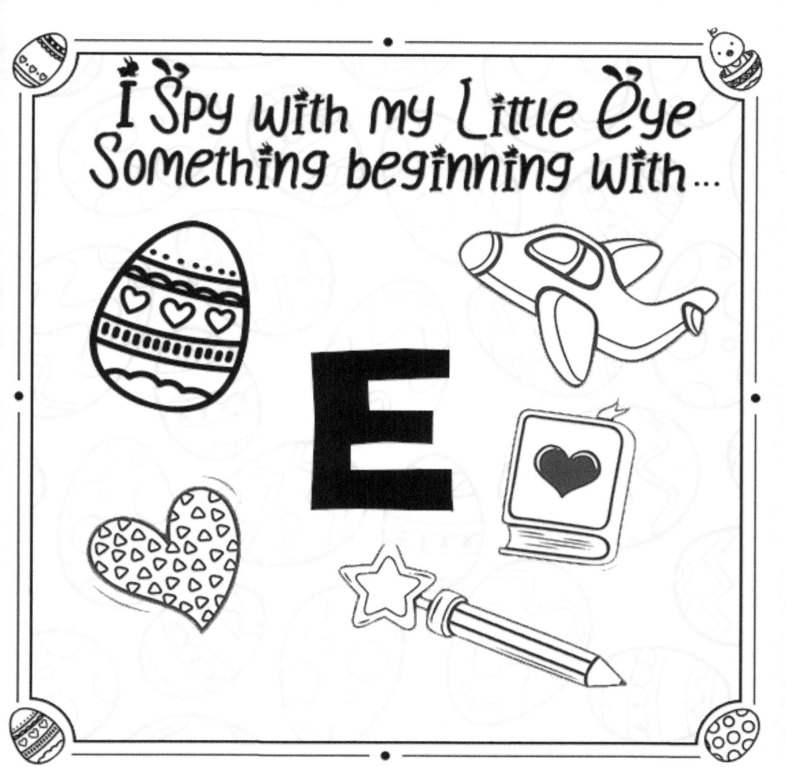

I Spied an

EGG

I Spied a

Flower

I Spied a

GRASS

I Spied an

HIPPOPOTAMUS

I Spied an

ICE CREAM

I Spied a

JAR

I Spied a

KANGAROO

I Spied a

LAMB

I Spied a

MOUSE

I Spied a

NECKLACE

I Spy with my Little Eye Something beginning with...

I Spied an

OCTOPUS

I Spy with my Little Eye Something beginning with...

I Spied a

PIANO

I Spied a

QUEEN

I Spied a

RABBIT

I Spy with my Little Eye Something beginning with...

I Spied a

SHOES

I Spy with my Little Eye Something beginning with...

I Spied a

TULIP

I Spy with my Little Eye Something beginning with...

I Spied an

UMBRELLA

I Spy with my Little Eye Something beginning with...

I Spied a

VAN

I Spied a

WATERMELON

I Spy with my Little Eye
Something beginning with...

I Spied a

XYLOPHONE

I Spy with my Little Eye Something beginning with...

Y

I Spied a

YARN

I Spied a

ZEBRA

Made in the USA
Middletown, DE
10 April 2022

63988077R00060